Ordinary

By Carol Anderson

The Puddin'head Press
2005

Additional copies of this book
may be ordered by writing to:

The Puddin'head Press
PO Box 477889
Chicago IL 60647
708-656-4900

www.puddinheadpress.com

Cover illustration by Carol Anderson

First Edition
2005

Library of Congress Control Number
2005905126

ISBN# 978-0-9724339-3-7

Dedication

To Ray G. Anderson,
who brought me to awareness of the wonder,
to Swede and Magee, to John Broehl,
to Mariah Crowley
who loved me into life,
and to all the ordinary humans who continue
to live and love, and teach me how.

When worries scratch our hearts,
when fear claws our minds,
when hells grab our souls,
it is then we rise and wash and dress
and go to work and tend the children
and pay the bills, do the dishes,
do the laundry, clean the house.

It is then,
in the doing of the ordinary,
we place ourselves
in the Ordinary of Worship
and heal our souls.

Carol Anderson

Acknowledgements

Acknowledgement is given for first publication of some of these poems to: The Aurorean, Dream International Quarterly, Offerings, and UpSouth.

Special acknowledgement to Michael Bugeja, John Dickson, Stanley Kunitz, Effie Mihopolous, Cora Moore, Gertrude Rubin, and Lawrence Tyler for their encouragement.

A most special acknowledgement of gratitude for his encouragement and his patience, belongs to my editor, David Gecic.

Table Of Contents

Ordinary

Crossing Alone

She followed him as he walked the sterile fields
hoping to retrieve the onion skins he shed
knowing she could not, would not,

cautiously stepping over and around
translucent skin where it fell;
and, when the field ended
at the bar she could not cross,
he climbed over and turned to her
and she saw his deep inner core,

sweet and desirable and hot with his pain.

Ordinary Taste

Crisp tangy sweet or soft sugary strong
raw or fried
or ringed and French fried
or best of all
fried into a loaf
or better than best
the blooming onion
with dipping sauce

such an ordinary taste
I'm told

Well, yes – ordinary as the rich earth
and the sun and the wind and the rain
but no roast beef sandwich seems complete
without a slice of raw onion
and what is a hamburger without grilled onions
a hot dog without them diced

Salads without their essence
are bland and useless
rather like eating water with tomatoes
and people know
no Irish stew
can be made
without
an
onion

White, Yellow, Purple, Green
colors as myriad as shapes and sizes
tastes as different as Vidalia
to Bermuda
to crunchy fire

even the reconstituted
dehydrated chopped onions
of a certain
fast food chain
are perfect in their own
ordinary way

all ordinary taste for
ordinary onion loving
me

Abuser and Abused

He drums dark thoughts
into her naive mind;
how dumb she is,
how foolish, and how bad;
bombarding her
with brutal words, beetle
brow, upraised hand,
sneering at her true goals,
until she finds

that when he stops and waits,
she then is glad
to sob her "Sorries"
from her beaten soul.

He draws her near,
he mouths faked sympathy;
he feeds her, tells her
he'll make things all right.

All she should do,
he says,
is what she knows
he wants.
The house, the sex,
the empathy
with his wishes and his needs.
Day and night,
do things his way.

She gives him full control
of her friends,
her phone calls,
her job,
her walks,
her clothes,
the color of her lipstick.

Even, now, lets him
control
her breath,
until, at last, she finds
he only wants
her death.

Let Me Not Go There

I am not afraid of places
where the dead now lie
buried, marked,
gone

once I played in the graveyards

Oakwoods Cemetery, great
for hide and seek
for collecting tree toads
St. Mary's great for tag
and word games made
from prayers engraved
upon the stones

still today I will walk the shaded loveliness
of little Sacred Heart Cemetery
set neatly in amongst the ancient oaks
of the forest preserve

I will fish the lagoon out back
in Resurrection Cemetery
where there lives
an old and honored
humongous small mouth bass

no, I do not fear the places
where the dead now lie
buried, marked, gone

but there are places I do not wish to go
which draw me back, hold me in their air
the fields around the town
outside the cemetery
of Gettysburg, Pennsylvania
those fields with simple stones
New York Number such and such artillery
        three hundred five men
                one hundred twenty-four dead
                        forty-nine wounded
                                thirty-seven missing

over and over across the fields
upon the gentle meadows
fencing the cornfields the hay rows
the stones
forty-fourth regiment Alabama Fusiliers
        two hundred eighty men
                two hundred thirty-one dead
                        forty-two wounded,
                                three captured
                                        four missing

and the blood soaked land
dry this century and more
grabs at me, sucks my feet
holds my air

grabs at me and holds

I am not afraid of the places
where the dead now lie
buried, marked, gone
yet there are places I do not wish to go
places where
God willing
I will never go

the beaches of Normandy
over the sunken hull of the Arizona
or the Utah in Pearl Harbor
that entire bay
the killing fields of Cambodia
the forest of Verdun

I am not afraid of the places
where the dead now lie
buried, marked, gone

yet, God help me,
there are places where
I do not wish to go
where my trembling skin
might not hold

if the gentle farming grounds outside that tourist town
of Gettysburg, Pennsylvania
could grab at me, hold me so

my God, what would happen
if I should breathe the air
at Auschwitz, The Twin Towers, or Dachau

I fear to drive, let alone walk
The Trail of Tears

there are mountain spots which held me
and I did not know
what had happened there

but they are places where the earth still cries
and the feel of blood is near
yet because I was there
they call me back
and grab my air

I can not go, God
don't let me go
to the places where your soil
holds the blood
of so many…

I am not You
I cannot suffer so

Cease Fire

Cease fire, she thought
as she buried her head
in her arms

Stop shooting the mortars
directly into my path
let them fall into a hole
somewhere else where I won't have
to dig through the debris
when the pile
topples
pick up those who are left
including myself
rummage through the rubble
to find some solid bricks

and try once again
to build something strong
from the wreckage
something able
next time around
to stand up to
falling hell

she uncovered her head
and moved through the dust
towards the wracked building
where yesterday her neighbors
lived and worked and played

Cease fire, she prayed
or hoped she did
for she could no longer hear

Miscarriage

No cigars handed out today, only a measure
of misery, of lost hope, of joy evaporated
with the cleared away fetus, the placenta,
the blood. Only the clear memory of footprints
from within her tapping his back, of tickle
of rolling wiggles and then of the sudden
terrifying vortex when all movement ceased
and he knew even as she awoke crying out
"Something's wrong," that their infant died.

He held her, carried her, called the doctor,
rushed her to the hospital but they knew
in their skins' souls that the child she carried
within had left only a form behind and their
arms would never hold this particular
measure of their love,
knew the months and years to come
would always feel the absence on the skin
of the child who left before the birth.

Swede and Magee

His name was Charles Crowley. They called him Swede.
Her name was Margaret Hughes. They called her Magee.
The gossips whispered "That marriage will never last."

Magee she was eighteen and carefree and gay
He was twenty-nine, already once divorced,
And the crease in his slacks, they said
Could cut butter on a hot summer's day.

No one could foresee the troubles which waited,
The illnesses which would stalk their family
Nor could they have dreamt just how stalwart they'd prove.
Through the depression, for neighbors in need,
For all of their lives holding open their hearts,
Sharing that stuff that 'could never last'.
Magee was nurse to the neighborhood. When others' needs
Called her away from their home, Swede cooked and cleaned
And tended the children after his day at work.
They took in forty children, without paperwork or pay,
For varying times; children whose folks had hit hard times,
Disappeared, or died.
Had seven children of their own when Swede got cancer
And went to Hines.
Even then Marge took in two who were left alone,
The young boy Billy and his sister Joan
So on the day Swede died
Nine were left for Magee
To raise alone.

Twenty-one years of loving and giving
was what came from Swede and Magee
That Crowley couple they said
"Will never last."

Hands

They were different, those hands of Swede, and Magee.

My father, Swede, his hands were beautiful to see
Long and slender and tapered thin
Death ridged nails as clean as new baby's skin
Whether he worked at the gas station or the mill.

My mother, Magee, her hands broad, thick, strong.
I remember the span of her fingers
French polished nails, clean and long
Twisting water from clothes after the wringer.

The knuckles, quite different, but not the love
In the reproving slaps, the gentle strokes,
Hard palms on both, both calloused rough.

Oh give me one wish. Let me once again feel
The tough love touch of Swede and Magee

After an Argument with His Teen

He searched through the stretched and twisted hours
of the night, night of the designer wind who
decorated, dismantled, tore down,
and renovated streets of locked doors,
fenced windows, and miniscule yards.
He searched each street, cursing the wind,
searched the alleys where naked and aged
lilac bushes shoved shivering arms through
fences of wood, or brick, of linked chain.

He linked his eyes to each slender form
huddled in coats against the willful wind
and some were El Greco's he dismissed
and others were sad eyed Keene's, but none
bore the spark of anger which twisted, flew
against the fence posts of his mind
nor reached with sorrow and mending voice
to soothe the word scratches in his soul
or maybe pivot and scratch some more
cutting another crack into his mind.

He stomped his feet on cracked cement
moved the search as he divided the blocks
and marched the alleys with drill precision
eyes left, eyes right, eyes forward, onward
while the wind screeched obscenities,
and the aged night wore on
until he slogged with dogged trudge,
no longer hoping, for he could not see
through freezing tears which found
their own reckless course, outward, down
the streets and alleys of his face.

Wind pushed him into a sheltered alley where
he found a family huddled asleep in their car,
a teal colored 1992 Ford, where they lived together
and further down the block another group
shivering snores from a Dell Computer box.
He met some wild-eyed ones strung out to where
they saw Bin Laden and Lucifer in the doors.
He turned the corner, and a calico cat
stared down the street, heedless of him,
from the window of a red brick bungalow
and he recalled an angry night when he deposed
his parents from their rightful place
as the counselors of him,
left a similar bungalow,
a teen sated with pride.

Pride had carried him far from the boy he'd been,
and this child of his heart with whom he fought,
was caught in the web between child and adult.
He pondered as he stood on the wind painted street
knowing he'd gone too far, forgotten too much,
said words that seared, words that cut,
words which sent him to this desolate spot
Now he longed for the touch of his father's hand.

A touch that was gone to the burial plot
with the smiles and grins and the tears and the fight.
He sorrowed now that they had never again
come to friendship as father and son.
He whispered "I love you," into the wind,
and turned his feet homeward, knowing
that what he had lost
he must find within.

Rhapsody of and in The Ordinary

Sun scalloping the condo roofs as morning rises
Rain shimmering fallen, browning leaves
Drift of fog sifting outlines into dreaming haze
Or snow suffusing day's light into a Monet
Ordinary weather for ordinary days.
I live in the ordinary, joy in the ordinary.

Ordinary hours of work and play, of gentle
Shout and tickling touch, of the day of now
When we have so much. This now. This ordinary
Shining second of this ordinary minute of this
Ordinary hour of this ordinary day.

Moments of scuffling feet through fallen leaves
Of glory shout from golden tawny maple trees
Of staid oaks in maroon dress and umber hose
Waiting to slumber the winter days away
Of children playing and a young voice chanting
"God is bigger than the bogey man."

Scenes of dirty dishes waiting to be washed
Of the food that filled them in an ordinary way
As we ate and were stilled and held the taste
Of joy in the ordinary meal cooked by an ordinary
Human on this ordinary glory, extraordinary day.

I was born in the ordinary way
Will die in some ordinary way
And joy in the ordinary in between.

New Year's Day 2005 Birth Of A Poem

Simple task, chauffeuring a friend
To Border's Book Store
in Orland

so he could use spend
his Christmas gift
of a gift certificate

struck as I waited
by a photograph
on the cover of a book

laughing servicemen
and smiling women
crowding State Street

on the date of August
fourteenth, 1945
ambushed by memory surge

Dick Simmons leaning from
the second floor window
yelling the war is over

baseball bat, mitts, ball
tossed aside to land
in Mrs. Halls' front yard

roller skates tugged off
slung around necks
with the skate keys

herding and migratory
instinct operating our block
as from every door

the maroon brick six flats
the white frame single family
homes, the red brick bungalows

even from the corners'
anchoring twenty-four flat
buildings and the Ruthmere Hotel

from the Drexel Arms
to the two flats
they trickled poured

mothers grandmothers aunts
a very few older fathers
and uncles joined with grandfathers

slipping on hats as they hobbled
out to join the women wiping
washing baking reddened hands

on house dresses or mickey aprons
untying simple aprons
slipping them over fences

over hedges as they walked
some north to Drexel Bible Church
some south to Holy Cross Catholic Church

we children following silently
wonder growing our happiness inside
as we watched our relatives

followed their lead
a few thank you thank you thank yous
stitched the air

someone maybe Mrs. O'Leary
she who had only two sons
left of three

and maybe only one
the second, Tommy, missing in action
said softly two simple words

Our Father
and the sound swelled until
the whole block hummed

in both directions on the block
the prayer over and over
carrying us up the steps

through the heavy carved doors
of our churches
where we knelt

and prayed
and cried
and heard

the happy click
of rosary beads
as the church

bloomed in light
from candles lit
with grocery money

with pennies saved
for a new skate key
or a comic book

and the bells rang
and someone sang
Holy God We Praise

Thy Name and faltering
at first we slowly joined in
until the walls rang

inside the story
which accompanied the picture
which triggered

all that memory
was a squib towards the end
of the second column

relating the lighting
of a candle
18 feet high

in the yard
at 2230 Washington
Boulevard

that squib the seed
from whose stem
grew these words

and a poem
entitled
Victory Candle

Victory Candle

(for J. A. Beauparlant)

How did he make it
with paraffin so hard to come by?
A normal candle, even one of three feet
would have been enough.
This, eighteen feet buffing
the sky, must have used
the work lives of many bees
or the kitchen canning wax
of many wives

So tall
he had to climb a ladder
to light it, that day,
that warm summer day
14th day of August,
nineteen hundred and forty-five

Two thousand two hundred
fifty pounds of wax
towering eighteen feet tall.

Three months of his life
the gathering of the wax
burnt candle ends perhaps
from neighbors who knew
his fierce fiery concentration
as a nagging abomination
and gave their leavings
to be rid of the strangeness
perhaps begging of all the farmers
he met at the market
the honeycomb from the hive

Likely pestering his wife until
his constant melting
his one minded will
seethed her kitchen

he would make a victory candle
melt the wax
build it with his hands around

the wick – how did he make that wick?
What was its thickness? Was it found
string braided or twisted round and round
or rope from the carriage shed
which held the car up on blocks
until rationing tumbled down
somehow he did it, created it,
and that warm day
climbed the ladder
when war's end was announced

lit it.

Chicago Calendar

it has been
decreed officially now
the homeless are not to use park benches

it has been decreed officially now
homeless people are not to use the el

or subways for a place to thaw and sleep
(we already know
they're unwelcome
on Lower Wacker Drive)

however, these
people routed from CTA routes will be
handled humanely
we are assured
by those civilians
hired by politicians

the lures
held out are interviews
with social service
workers
temporary shelter at least
and possibly
a final solution.

seems to me I've heard that term before

Gravy Boat
(for Raymond Carver)

Hope the few lifts
I've given
have helped
tilt this
gravy boat
enough to allow
the gravy
to flow
over others
as it's poured
out for me
these past
years

sixteen plus
years
of pure
wonderful
rich brown
tasty gravy

now I must
remember
to eye the gravy boat
for those minute cracks
of age
and repair it
with tradition

so it remains
plain white
simple
gravy boat
for the ages

The Shooting

They were laughing, walking in the winter sun
on new white snow when the drive by began
her son sheltered mom, shoved her down
she felt his weight lighten, knew he was gone

someone was screaming inside her head
she pushed herself up, tugged his empty shell
cradled it and rocked it in arms stained red
and the pale sun fell on that anguished hell

they eased his shredded body from her arms
helped her up, wrapped her in a blanket warm
walked her away, though she tried not to go
she fell… hand clawing through the bloodied snow

at Mercy Hospital they gave her medicine
tried to open her hand, phoned her husband
here are pills, keep her warm, you both sleep
you've been through hell and rest is what you need

her husband whispered, his voice torn and low
say, doctor, why won't she unclench her fist?
reflex action, they said... they couldn't know
she clutched one shriveled fragment

of their son's flesh.

The Reason Why

Forty years we've raced
in mess and clutter and fun.
Other prizes gained ascendance
over neatness; reading, laughter,
dances, football, living in
and making love.

Now you scratch your head, wonder
why suddenly I trot, snatch up dirty clothes,
dry dishes, put away laundry, stack
magazines and newspapers, make
your life a torment with the neatness.

I'll tell you, this reasoning that came,
the reason why.

The seasons gallop lately.
Our races became pasture years too soon.
I would have no shame
        (when the hearse must come)
for the one whom
must lap the course alone.

Hear My Call

Through golden prairie grasses
standing tall above the snow
Can you hear my love
calling clear to you

Through the salted city streets
over mounds of graying snow
Can you hear my love
calling clear to you

From the floor where I sat
beside my father's feet
Did you hear then my love
whispering for you

At the paper stand on Drexel
where you washed my face in snow
Did you suddenly then know
my love was laughing on to you

From Lackland Air Base in San Antonio
where your basic was performed
Did you know then my love
would be calling clear to you

At Luke Air Base
through the letters pouring through
There I know you heard my love
calling clear to you

Then across the sea in Seoul
I'd like to let you know
that I heard then the love
calling clear from you

You came back to Chicago
where our love called to its own
where we moved on together
heard our love calling clear

Through our children and the years
of mistakes and fun and joy and fear
we worked to hold the promise
of our love calling clear

And now across the bend of space
across the light trails of the years
I pray you hear the faint trace
of my love calling clear

From the pain within my soul
from this deep hard need to know
I ask you to listen, and to hear
my love calling on, calling clear

Oh hear my long dead man,
across the bounds of God
my love calling clear to you

Beloved

Beloved is an old fashioned word, term
of endearment which says be loved by me
in all the forms which love may gently give

Be loved, my beloved, when I take time
to find your body fine and beautiful
be loved, beloved, when I say your mind
is quirky and witty and bountiful
be loved, beloved, when I feel pain
for each and every one of your scars
be loved, beloved, for who you are
with all your failings, your faults, beloved
be loved because each is a part of you
and in whole or in part, entire or flawed
they are sweet hope and abiding awed faith
in what has grown in me since I was blessed
to be so very beloved of you
of you.

To Ray with Love

This is where I must go now
this strange outer world
where people live and love and laugh
and do real things
while I do not belong
for life has left with you
and love has gone forever
to wherever you have gone
though I laugh still and sometimes cry
pretending that I'm real

if all we had was a staged act
and this is what is real
I am an open hollow
tucked between the hills of life
and no road or path can I find
that shows me a way out

unmade beds or beds tucked up
dishes waiting or already washed
floors need sweeping
plants need water
and only this unreal being
left to do the tasks

so I move again grab my coat
rattle the car keys and flee
to someplace else where no one knows
the unreality of
me

quiet now, it's quiet now

It's quiet now
they've all gone home
they wrapped all that food
crammed our refrigerator
washed the glasses
and tableware
lugged out the garbage bags
stuffed with paper plates
and congealed potato salad

they've gone home
leaving behind their parting words
"Let us know if there's anything
anything at all
we can do."
they've all gone home

it's quiet now
too quiet
I hear the candles guttering out
along the fence
the dry petals of flowers
piled along the sidewalk
rustle loudly
but there is no snick
of refrigerator door
no voice calling
"What's to eat?
Look what I got!"
no plop of book bag
on the floor

it's quiet now
no shatter pop of gunfire
no shouted gang slogans
no police sirens
tear apart the silence
no squealed last call of "Mama"
no running footfalls
no peel of rubber
pull my fear to find your bloodied form
emptied of laugher and warmth

it's quiet now
no more hymns of your classmates
no "Amens" can hide His words
"Forgive us our trespasses
as we forgive
those who trespass against us!"

it's quiet now
I can hear
the screaming
of
my soul

Kaddish for The USS Cole

What verses are Kaddish, Lord?
Or the rites for the dead?
I would say them for those sailors
men and women in safe harbor
or so they thought, when without a word
they were torn apart, split more surely
than lambs led to slaughter
for those too soon shortened lives
my soul voices Kaddish with its tears

Their families... how can we comfort
across this nation those so bereft
what shoulder can we offer broad enough
what comforting arm long enough
to stretch to those in Texas
North Carolina, Florida
Wisconsin, Georgia.
North Dakota, California
Mississippi, Virginia
Maryland and Pennsylvania?

And I, a sinner, dare not ask
for justice
but only mercy on us all.

A Rose Patterned Quilt

Flattened of all its once proud puffiness,
scarlet roses and dark green stems lightened
to red outlining pink with faint
yellow green leaves and thorns,
the quilt sits at the bottom of the daybed.
Its under-scarlet still blazes the edge
almost as though it fluffed
upon the double bed high above the floor
which sheltered our spooned selves,
almost as though it covered us
with new love growing,
with all the promise of years
still to unfold.

"Why don't you get rid of that old thing?"
they ask when they visit.
"We remember it from when we were kids.
Why don't you toss it, let us give
you something new and bright and warm?
There's no filling left there, it must harm
your arthritis to be so cold."
They do not add and so old.

That quilt sheltered us
when it was young, down-fluffed,
bright, and warm.
Still, somehow, it holds
an essence of us,
though one is gone
and the other is whitened,
wrinkled and alone.

Alphabet After September 11th

All around
below burnt buildings
come the corpses

deformed, destroyed
etherized eternals
floating free.

Gray grit
hovers here.

Innocents, ink
juxtaposed, joined.
Kindling killed.

Lovers of life
miss mornings
noons
now.

Over open
places

people paste
quick, quiet
remnants, reminders.

Soft sobs
toll the truth.

Undulations urge the
valiant to verify
wreaked wreckage of

war.

Xenophobic
youths yawp
zealot's zeal.

cool water

(for Lawrence Tyler)

once you thought it was Christ calling
"Red rover, red rover, let him come over"
later, with Scotty,
at his great grandmother's wake
as he called "Wake up, Grandma, wake up,"
you wondered if it was all
just that simple
was Christ simply calling to us
"Wake up, wake up?"

at the end when you were too weak
or too confused to write poetry
still you tried, you pretended
and before you ended
that pretense
you said
"the words are cool water"

I need to believe
you've found it all at last
Christ called you to come over
and you went
and awakened
to the joy
of living waters

drink deeply
joy, enjoy,
joy
my friend
some God time
we'll meet again

random thoughts on the war

Thrusts of red orange climbing to meet
spiked darts of white death coming in
buildings collapsed into dusty rubble
and the cost routinely called out
over the air, five hundred scud
missiles at a cost of one million
dollars each.

A new war will go on the war memorial
in the small Illinois town of St. Anne
where the Beaupre boy will not return
Captain Beaupre flew his last helicopter
flight into Kuwait, crashing, with eleven
others on board; no one has mentioned
the cost: twelve young men at a cost
of what for each.

And the stock market climbed again,
soared high and promises to go further.
War, it would seem, will benefit someone.

For J.J. Jameson

The acorn landing on tannin soaked earth
cannot imagine the sapling
bent and twisted by unimaginable wind
or seared by fire
cut by lightning
falling

the tortured sapling cannot know
whether the stretching towards the sky
standing against the wind
sending out new shoots after the fire
putting down some solid roots

will let it grow or not

the steadfast oak
weather-scarred trunk
striated bark
life twisted limbs

remembered the acorn the sapling
lifted its aching limbs to praise
to shelter
to reach the sun
to uphold new growth
until it too could see the sky

it cannot know it will hear the whisper
inasmuch as you did it for one of these
you have done it also unto me

Thank you J.J. for being for a time
a steadfast oak for many

Christened

for David Gecic

Not that the water poured, the salt tipped,
the words blessed; still I was christened
that cloudsung day by the outpouring
of your laughter, the tiptilt of your quiet hug,
the unspoken blessing of your compassion.

One Day in a Bedroom

Nine A. M.
The room emptied now of furniture.
Changing table gone,
youth bed removed,
and now, the real bed.
Shining cherry, with drawers beneath
to hold linens, blankets, treasures.
The father labors, setting it up,
moves in the chest of drawers,
makes the bed,
replaces Pooh Bear and Tigger
on the pillow.

Ten A. M.
The father peers in the room
as he passes the door.
Pooh Bear is kicked under
the chest of drawers,
Tigger lies discarded
upside down in a corner.
Horses and cowboy hat
and a wrestler action figure
recline upon the bed.
Rounded wooden cars and
train tossed in the closet,
sleek and shining
matchbox cars dot the floor
and the father does not know
why he stands in the doorway
crying.

Noon

Always, when doing the laundry,
the mother thinks of those who wear
these clothes;
sees the growth
in length of pants and skirts,
notes the change in type
of dirt and stain.
Laundry shows reality
of toddler growing into boy,
teen-aged daughter
becoming woman.
And so she is unprepared
for the sob that catches her throat
as she carries jeans and tee shirts,
shorts and socks,
into the room where yesterday
a youth bed sat with Pooh Bear
and Tigger on the pillow.

Nine P.M.

The woman leans into
the man's shoulder, his arm
encircles her waist.
Light from the hall roams past
strikes the red haired boy
sleeping in the bed,
right hand clutching a horse.
The father points to the bulges
next to the boy, under the blanket,
and the caramel colored paw
and orange and black tail
hanging out the side.

Given Song

This morn in my head a place name rung
A place called Cullyghillin
And if it's real this song is sung
In hopes it will stop the killin'
And if in fact it's just a dream
And the woman I saw who was cryin'
The words that follow were very real
She was trying to stop the dying

And she cried:

"And is it to begin again
The bloodshed and the fear
The shutting down of opened hearts
The burying of those who're dear

"The burying it must be done
Yet our hearts held open still
For it's not those I've come to love
Who've come here and done this kill

"But a terrorist from here or there
Still a terrorist nonetheless
Yet I'll live in peace with all people here
Even though one should confess

"That he or she were a terrorist
Who helped do this awful thing
So 'Down with all the terrorists!'
We Irish women sing.

"Try them, and pity them.
And pray for their souls,
For nourished they were on hate,
But oh, for these little ones
Whom we hold
Let love not be too late."

This morn in my head a place name rung
A place called Cullyghillin
And if it's real this song is sung
In hopes it will stop the killin'
And if it's not, let this be a prayer
That love will hold tight and fast
That all the people in all the places
Will live in peace at last.

"Down with all the terrorists!"
Let people of the world state.
"Try them, and pity them,
and pray for their souls,
for nourished they were on hate.
But oh, for these little ones
Whom we hold
Let love not be too late."

After We Get Off Our Knees, What Then?

On September 11th we were assaulted
by the cowardly horrors of hell.
We shuddered to find that evil lives,
that evil is a reality stark and strong,
and the world watched in horror
with us, certain we must fall.

Yes, fall we did;
fell to our knees in prayer,
though in our hearts hatred rose.
Still a voice we knew as children whispered
"Hating is evil, evil is hatred.
Be still and know that I am God."
We listened there on our knees in prayer,
then stood, and worked to do what we could;
help in the digging,
give our blood,
send our money,
and pray.

"But when we get off our knees," we asked,
"what do we do then?"

We do what we saw those heroes do.
We walk our prayer into work.
We tend to the duties of our daily lives
and we give until it hurts.

We awaken to grief so heavy we're sure
there's no way we can move;
yet still we rise, in spite of bleeding minds,
to tend our children with love.

We hand a sandwich to a hungry man;
we bring a blanket to the homeless;
we fly our flags within our working hands
and we work together for justice.

We get rid of the drug dealers, the lawless guns,
the evil thugs who prey on our kids.
We teach our children right from wrong

and we grieve over our honored dead.

That's prayer that works, and work that is prayer,
and it can, and will overcome horror;
for love is good, and our God is love;
and always love overcomes evil.

Though never easily.
The road will be hard
the journey, rugged and tiring;
but, "Hear us, Oh God,
in spite of all hell,
from now on You'll find us trying----

trying our American best
to walk our love into prayer."

Quest for The Grail

To walk and to judge the might of battling wind
to listen for birds' soaring trill as they wing
on their way to the day and the glory thereof;
this is to ask.

To kneel, to grope for words in a battered mind,
to ache in despair's deep hole as prayer flits
irrelevantly from dreams to sins perceived;
this is to seek.

To inch forward against wind's tormenting might,
to ignore the rattling mind, with coarsened voice
croak long buried hymn, herald anthem of praise;
this is to knock.

To struggle beyond wind to the place of quiet
is to receive;
to pray through the tumult to the place of peace
is to find.

To praise in hell, bury ego, merge with all,
is to hear
"Now, see the door is opened unto you. Come,
drink from the Grail."

Done for Today

Done. As much and far more than I expected
and the price has been high;
but, why would I expect otherwise
when sloth was all I reflected
for all of this past year?
I would like to murmur
that this was not my fault.
I would like to poor me
for a day or two without guilt.
Ouch. That is clearly not to be
for though the work is,
almost, all done;
though help came when I asked,
it has been a rigorous task.

Yes, I expect,
when at last
all is done

I will be all in.

Me, Myself and I

Everywhere I go I find
that somehow I am three
for where I am there also are
both myself and me.

I begin writing. Suddenly
I find me is striking the keys,
myself is saying, "Dump that word!"
(She is extremely hard to please.)

When shopping me hunts solid worth
but I am after flair and dash
and we get hit with great letdowns
for myself won't part with the cash.

Food presents another problem
for oh, I truly love to eat,
though me is always dieting,
and myself wants only what's sweet.

I cook great feasts, just for I
but me, myself eat, say "Delicious,"
yet half an hour later they can't be found
when it is time for washing the dishes.

Me is a fraidy cat, and shy.
Myself jumps into any fray.
Sitting, watching, conservative I
works on serenely through the day.

And now I'm done, not even sure
of who is writing this. For see,
I thought t'was I, until myself
announced that it was me.

Ordinary of Worship

To be deeply flawed
become a Lizzie Borden, Jack the Ripper

    To be so grievously cleft
    as to be a John Gacy, a Hitler

To be so perfectly healed
become a Francis of Assisi, Catherine of Siena

    To be so love flamed
    as to be Jeanne d'Arc, Martin Luther King,
    or Mother Theresa

These are not our territory

For though we walk, soul wounded
we are only lightly scarred

now that He has healed us
with searing touch

so gentle we are but ordinary

and so we order this day's worship

ordinary
    extraordinary
        territory

of

His Hours

Search for You

Long, long have I sought You
yet could not find You
You who are without limits
and would not fit my outlines
but overflowed, engulfed
swallowed, swept over and through
every concept which I dreamt
every line that I drew

until the day I learned
the pain crabbed hand was Yours
the withered limbs held Your feet
Your eyes gazed out from a scarred face
and Your words ushered forth
from spittled lips

until I knew the milk sweet scent of infants
the sour puke odor of the drunkard
the stench of gangrenous flesh
and the sensual aroma of honest sweat
were all Your breath

until I knew the eyes whited out by blindness
crossed by lax muscles
alert and scintillating in every color
were all Your eyes

until I knew You lived
in me
I could not find You

Dichotomy

"Eli, Eli, lama sabachthani?"
Despairing cry of God's dichotomy.

"My God, my God,
        Why have you forsaken me?"
My cry is answered
By God's humanity.

About the Author

Carol Anderson was born and raised on the south side of Chicago. At the age of two she developed a bone disease which immobilized her in bed for the next three years. There, her grandmother read to her fairy tales, Aesop's Fables, and poetry, her index finger moving under each word. Robert Louis Stevenson's 'Land of Counterpane' spoke directly to the bedridden child, ignited a passion for poetry which continues to this day.

Carol Anderson has had her work published in numerous literary journals including: The Aurorean, Cappers, Dream International Quarterly, Grit, Guideposts, Red Owl Magazine and Upsouth. She has had her non-poetic work published in Guideposts and Streetwise.